There's No Danger in the *Water*

Encouraging Black Men To Become Mentors

Dr. Belay D. Reddick, Sr.
written with Danquirs Franklin

authorHOUSE®

AuthorHouse™
1663 Liberty Drive
Bloomington, IN 47403
www.authorhouse.com
Phone: 1-800-839-8640

Published by AuthorHouse 8/8/2013

ISBN: 978-1-4817-5186-5 (sc)
ISBN: 978-1-4817-5185-8 (e)

Library of Congress Control Number: 2013908401

Dedication

To my children, De'Andre, Belay II and Brianna, with thanks for inspiring me, for the generosity of their love, and for allowing me to share their lives with others as precious gifts I have always known they were.

Dr. Belay D. Reddick, Sr.

To my daughter, Skyy Lee, that she might never settle for substandard.

Danquirs Franklin

Acknowledgements

There's No Danger in the Water makes book number one for us. We're proud of that. We are more proud of the fact that we were able to collaborate on this book miles away from one another. This is only a testimony of how awesome God is.

To the good people of AuthorHouse Publishing, especially our senior publishing consultant, Tim Murphy, who were tremendously helpful in seeing this project through.

Special thanks to Teresa Scott-Pickens and Richard "Slick Rick" Adderson, our extended family, who made this book and its contents possible. Much love and respect.

Thanks to the invaluable contribution of William A. Briscoe, who typed this manuscript and provided enormously helpful suggestions and ideas; and his sidekick Robert Goldstein.

We are especially thankful for Deborah Franklin and Mary Boyd, who allowed us the opportunity to build a true friendship. And finally, we are grateful to Eric Frazier of the Charlotte Observer for connecting our lives together through his pen.

Contents

Why We Need Black Male Role Models

I don't have to be a professor of economics or a political pundit to see these are absolutely the worst of times in the United States, the most powerful country in the world. The economy is bad. More than 14 million remain jobless. States are seeking to save money by beefing up probation and parole programs to reduce the number of prison inmates, as well as pushing rehabilitation over jail for low-level drug crimes. While national unemployment stands at about 9.2 percent, black unemployment is 16.2 percent. It's 17 percent for black men. Scores of families are facing home foreclosures. Another factor that speak to both the economic competitiveness and security of America - the K-12 public education system - is also in crisis.

For President Obama, it's personal. For the country it's critical. For black America, it's the civil rights issue of the 21st century. For me, it's morally unacceptable. We know that the bedrock and fuel of American innovation and success is a quality education, which leads to opportunity, higher salaries, safer communities, and a stronger nation. And every parent, regardless of race, nationality, or economic status, wants their child to have the best possible education.

Nationwide, three out of 10 students never graduate. In some inner city schools, only three out of 10 do. What's troubling about these numbers is that 12 percent of the schools produce 50 percent of America's dropout rates. Yet, no one wants to do what it takes to make the changes necessary for America to reclaim its position as the best educated nation on the planet. We can gather all the panels of experts we want to discuss solutions for our ailing public school system, but if the solutions don't address the causes, high school dropouts will continually be condemned to poverty and social failure.

At a time when the American educational system is broken, the United States poverty rate remains among the highest in the developed world, and the country has a $15 trillion debt, our elected representatives seem more interested in playing politics and pointing fingers.

Problems in Europe no doubt are heading our way. If this country and especially our elected officials don't toughen up and make some hard choices, we are in a mess in the next few years. Indeed, as I write this book, the so-called "supercommittee" charged with cutting the deficit before Thanksgiving just $1.2 trillion over ten years - had to admit abject failure. The Republicans have been unified for two decades in opposition to higher taxes, while the Democrats on the committee were insisting on additional revenue before they agreed to cuts in benefit programs such as Medicare.

Congress continues to prove itself irrelevant and incapable in the effort to get the country's fiscal house in order. Many will agree this 112th Congress ought to resign in sheer mortification of being the worst excuse for a legislative body this nation has ever seen. The Republicans refusal to raise taxes on the rich, and willingness to cut them even below their current bargain-basement level has been a long-standing point of party orthodoxy. Washington claims Democrats refuse to budge on entitlements. House Speaker John Boehner and Republican presidential candidate Mitt Romney, as if by rote, issued statements saying it was all President Obama's fault. But, if a single Republican on the panel endorse even a modest increase in upper income tax rates, Republicans can win trillions in cuts from entitlements and discretionary spending. Soon or later, we will pay for the opportunities missed in 2011.

Right now, investors are contending with a market that offer both peril and panic. There is an increasing sense of nervousness with shareholders because of the latest meltdown on Wall Street. Despite the debt ceiling compromise, Standard & Poor's downgraded the United States a notch from the highest credit rating AAA to AA+. This unfortunate downgrade of our great nation has caused investors to change their view of the country.

As Occupy Wall Street protesters clog streets and tie up traffic in more than 100 U.S. cities, we debate in barbershops and beauty parlors whether this is a movement, or a series of events populated by a weird cast of disaffected characters; indeed they have an amorphous anger aimed at banks, investors, rich people and bourgeois values. The majority of those who back the Occupy movement simply want to restore a sense of fairness to this nation. Thanks to the Occupy Wall Street, we're talking more about greed, class inequality and corporate corruption.

Those who still have jobs in the private sector are too often finding themselves doing the work of two or three people with no more compensation than they received for doing the job of one person. The truth to the matter is that many CEOs and other corporate executives are so grossly overpaid that they could easily take pay cuts that would release funds to help hire other people and still not feel any great economic pinch.

What we have seen over the past decade in this country is a great imbalance in the distribution of wealth. The rich and powerful continue to take a greater share while the poor and middle class continue to see their incomes and buying power fade away.

We need to re-establish this nation as being "of the people, by the people and for the people" rather than of the few, by the few and for the few. We must break the power of individuals such as Grover Norquist, president of Americans for Tax Reform, who has all Republican political candidates living in such fear that they feel they must sign his no-taxes pledge to gain or remain in political office.

While there are talks about breaking the status quo of excessive federal spending that is throwing our budget out of whack, we continue to see billions of dollars spent annually incarcerating and rehabilitating black boys for criminal and deviant behaviors. In 2009, the Bureau of Justice Statistics reported that nearly 70 percent of state and federal prisoners under the age of 24 were black males. The truth is, according to Frank Manfre, executive director of Boys to Men Mentoring of Georgia, "at-risk boys become at-risk men." I would add that at-risk men make at-risk babies.

Until society becomes aware of the fact that we must change the way we raise today's black boys, the vicious cycle of violence and murders will continue crippling our communities. It's true that slavery was bad. But we can't attribute all of our woes to the wrongs of the past. Many of our problems have been self-created. For example, roughly 30 percent of black children live in single-parent households headed by women. In 1920, 90 percent of black children had both parents at home. Projections are by the year 2050 there may not be one black family that has its father present. This is a clear indication that black America, despite its unparalleled achievement in sports, entertainment, politics and business is nowhere near completing the work started by those who sweated, bled, and died for us to get to where we are today. We must address the vital connection that is missing between black boys and black men.

If it sounds as if I'm trying to provoke a sense of urgency, I am. It's not enough to just raise black boys; we must raise black boys to become men who embrace personal responsibility.

Black boys need black men in their lives. It is said that only a man can teach a man how to be man. That speaks to the power of role models but more important is the mentoring that good black men can provide to black boys. Unfortunately, we have young black males who never met an African-American man willing to take them out of town, to a golf course, or even on a fishing trip. Congress can't solve this problem. We can.

One of the most reliable predictors of whether a black boy will succeed or fail in life rests on this question: Does he have a positive black male figure in his life to look up to? Too often, the answer is no. Sixty years ago, the greatest influence on black boys was the home, followed by school and church. Now, the greatest influences are peers, rappers and television. There have been numerous studies done by universities and national consultants that clearly prove whoever spends the most time with our children will have the greatest influence.

With each generation, black boys are moving away from their connection to mature masculinity, family and God. The sad fact is too many young black men are left trying to figure out manhood alone. In the words of Greek Author Aranna Huffington: "Not only is it harder to be a man, it is also harder to become one." Growing up without an active father, mentor or positive black male role model can have a devastating impact on an African-American boy.

Overcrowded penitentiaries, escalating gang affiliation and the dramatic increase in the number of fatherless homes are the visible top of the iceburg. We hear all the time stories of black boys growing up without fathers or living with disconnected or dysfunctional fathers.

We have disregarded all the evidence of black male achievement and ambition deficits and basically sat down as our boys have notched a growing record of failure and disengagement. It's time we stand up and do something about it.

Black boys don't need more history lessons, more tough talk or embarrassing; they need to be heard, appreciated, accepted and encouraged each day.

Black boys need black male role models and guidance to stay on the straight and narrow, a push to excel in athletics and extracurricular activities, help to develop a Wealth for Life Plan, recognition that they must be accountable to God and man for their actions, and reinforcement of best effort.

We have been idle long enough. Black boys need us. They need for us to listen to them. They need for us to ask them who they are. The answers they give may not always be clear, but talk to enough of them and we will discover that black boys themselves are not the problem. The problem is black men who step back instead of up. But it doesn't have to be that way. We can make a difference and reduce youth violence, dropout rates, and fatherless homes. It's not impossible to close the achievement gap between white and black boys.

Truth be told, we're not stepping into our leadership and vainly waiting for someone else to address this issue. Let's not bury another black boy before his time. We have to get out there and reach them before the penal system does. The harvest is huge - but there are only a few workers.

How A Prisoner Did It

L et me share with you the story of how I became a mentor. I'm sharing my story because too often our past transgressions seem worser than the next person's, so much so that we think we can't affect change. We don't know where to begin. Because we view the past transgressions as so bad, we think they require a special forgiveness from God as well. The fact is, no past transgression is too execrable or too defiling that it can't be pardoned. We simply need to get up and get going.

What makes Bill Cosby so special is that through his tough talks about values and responsibility he encourages black Americans to cleanse their culture, and reclaim the traditions that fortified them in the past. "No longer is a person embarrassed because they're pregnant without a husband. No longer is a boy considered an embarrassment if he tries to run away from being a father of the unmarried child," Bill Cosby expressed in one of his national call-out meetings.

The great abolitionist Frederick Douglass once said, "It is easier to build strong children than to repair broken men." It is the act of committing to a cause in which you believe, feeling that through your efforts you are making a difference. It's caring enough about the well-being of your community; eventually, your cause makes a difference.

On the field, a particular athlete can turn in a stellar performance that shows what an individual can do when we make an effort. In his illustrious fifteen year NFL career, Emmitt Smith rushed for a total of 18,355 yards, making him the leading lifetime rusher, eclipsing Walter Payton's record of 16,726 yards. What separated Emmitt Smith from other players is that he decided he was going to be the best in the game before the clock started. He always gave his best effort, even when he separated his shoulder in a game against the New York Giants. In doing so, he inspired a whole generation of children to "be like Emmitt." Some of those children - the Adrian Petersons and Maurice Jones-Drews of the world - came along to play after him, openly acknowledge that he had set the stage.

I was thirty-six years old when I found the person who set such a stage for me. Errol Thomas, one of the staff members at the Federal Correctional Institution in Edgefield, South Carolina, was brought up in a traditional Baptist church too. Young black males at the facility were always coming up to him with different personal matters that required immediate solutions. They had been left to puzzle out manhood alone. I saw the humbleness he had, the genuine sincerity he seemed to express in being able to respond to young men's problems and mentor them on a daily basis. Errol was the education technician at the Federal Correctional Institution, and ever day he would engage young black inmates in discussions about life. One day he invited me to attend their forum, making me a facilitator at age thirty-six.

Some time later, Rev. Larry Fryer of Augusta came to the Federal Correctional Institution for a Martin Luther King, Jr. program. As I heard him articulate why he was trying to reach a generation of troubled youth, I saw Rev. Fryer's determination and dedication toward making a difference. I was, at age thirty-six, sandwiched between one African-American man who was making a difference inside a prison and another African-American man who was making a difference outside a prison. Listening to them speak, I soaked up their message like a sponge.

As a result, I became a lifetime supporter of Fryer's cause to stop black-on-black violence. I remembered Fryer long after the program and continued to work with Errol. I was curious how he was able to win young black males over, and encourage them to live better lives. I didn't know of any other prison official at the Federal Correctional Institution that truly cared for the inmate population. What fascinated me was seeing Errol respond to young black men's questions. Fortunately for me, I worked for Errol as a tutor and spent a lot of time with him. I tagged along on errands as he collected overdue library books, talking to prisoners about their struggles and problems. I would sit in his office and go through inmate request forms. Errol treated me with respect, something that a man in a prison uniform didn't get all the time. I was at a point in my life where I was open to learning and responsibility, and I was soaking up everything he knew about today's black youth, seeing how they can be reached.

Now, Baptist folks believe in the Bible. The solution to everything is prayer. What I was reminded through hanging around Errol was that prayer doesn't take back our streets. We've got to do that ourselves. I grew up in a time when neighborhoods were much safer. We had very little killings. We were more loving, caring, and sharing, so I knew what it meant to have values.

I remember vowing to God that when I got out of prison, I would spend the rest of my life trying to do what Errol was doing, infusing young black men with a belief that, if they work hard and stay focused, they can achieve success. If Errol Thomas could make inroads with young black men, I could too.

Initially, my plan was to write urban street novels and become wealthy from prison like Vickie Stringer. After meeting Errol Thomas, I redirected my energies from writing fiction to writing nonfiction. I started educating myself on societal issues. My whole outlook changed.

After that, I published a monthly newsletter offering black clergymen across the country various strategies for stopping the vicious cycle of violence and murders that were crippling the African-American community. I wrote that increasing literacy rates was the best strategy. I believed one of the best ways to reduce the number of black boys in the penal system was to teach them how to read. Another prevention approach was for parents to spend more time with their children. At the time I met Errol, I didn't embrace mentoring and was not a conscious role model. But by the age thirty-seven I was volunteering to reach out to troubled black boys.

For example, when I heard about the number of high school students reported in Augusta being in a physical fight, and taking a gun or knife to school, I reached out to The Helen Blocker-Adams Show on WKZK 103.7. She dedicated a portion of her radio broadcast every Monday evening to air my letters with the youth. I encouraged young black males to stay in school, avoid anything that might put them behind bars and to never give up on hope. If they were headed down the wrong path, I pointed out exactly what changes had to take place in order for them to turn their lives around. It was a complete success, but the radio program cancelled.

In spring 2008, a friend of mine named Eric Frazier wrote a story in the Charlotte Observer about Midwood High and it's fight to reduce the dropout rate. After hearing the principal talk about her students' troubles, Frazier wondered if he could understand the challenges better by telling the story of one of them.

Fraizer requested to meet additional students. A small group showed up one morning in a conference room. Juwon Lewis, a black boy from the Villa Heights neighborhood, was among them.

Juwon Lewis stood out like a sore thumb. He was the only kid who brought his breakfast tray with him. The school officials informed Frazier he came to school hungry once in a while.

During numerous meetings covering more than a year, they talked about his life and future. During their initial dialogue one-on-one, Frazier asked if his mother was the only active parent in his life. He told him yes. Juwon was only seventeen.

Frazier wrote that his criminal record portrayed him a knucklehead at best, a thug at worst.

But Frazier took a liken to him. Others did, as well. Several teachers described his as intriguing. One went far enough to call him a natural leader. According to them, Juwon had this bona fide, mischievous coolness that, given the likelihoods he faced, made it difficult for you not to root for him.

Much later, Frazier ended up meeting his best friend, Danquirs Franklin, who attended Midwood the year before. They had grown up together, not to mention, faced similar difficulties.

Danquirs was born with cocaine in his body.

His mother smoked crack cocaine all nine months she carried him. Sometimes, Danquirs would see his mother walking the streets, jumping in and out of cars, and tell himself she was just another crack head. He was in denial. Danquirs very much needed her in his life because his father left him. Her absence made him furious.

Next door, Juwon's mother and grandmother spent most of their time in jail, generally on possession of crack cocaine charges. Crack cocaine and addicts were as much a part of his home as the kitchen sink. Whenever his mom and grandmother were sitting in a jail cell, he stayed down the street with "Miss Betty," his grandmother's friend. All his life, Juwon had been surrounded by drugs and addicts.

Both young men had no positive black male role model in their lives to guide them.

Together, their stories had shed more light on the troubles of fatherless black boys, perhaps the most imperiled group in America.

I wanted to believe my involvement with Juwon and Danquirs, despite being incarcerated, would be enough to impel them to finish school. So I did what I had to do.

I wrote both boys a letter in October 2010. Sadly, my efforts to reach both young men did not yield positive results. Juwon never responded to my letter. On November 11, days before his eighteen birthday, Juwon stopped going to school. That same month, the cops came to his house. They wanted to question Juwon about a number of burglaries. The next month, about a half-dozen cops pounded on his door again. This time, they wanted to question him about a stolen car. Although Juwon lived elsewhere, the unexpected visits had rattled Miss Betty. To this day, I believe Juwon could still turn things around if he had a positive black male role model in his life.

Before Christmas, I received a letter and card from Danquirs Franklin. He apologized for not writing me back much sooner. Danquirs had made peace with his past. He became a high school senior with hopes for college. His mother stopped using drugs and returned home. Danquirs thanked me for the letter, and wanted to know more about my life. In prison I didn't get those kinds of letters regularly. I usually received legal mail instead. That marked my first foray into the sphere of mentorship. For the first time in my life, I was out on the water of a real-life situation, volunteering to teach, to counsel, to reach out to a teenage black male with an inactive father.

My interests in Danquirs and his education brought me to the attention of his mother and grandmother. They called me a blessing, a compliment that encouraged me to continue what I had started. Danquirs and I never missed a Sunday talking to each other on the telephone.

In his senior year, Danquirs struggled to overcome the academic fallout from his deeply troubled childhood.

He had entered high school far behind his peers and couldn't write coherent sentences. I continued to encourage him not to give up through my letters and telephone calls. "You can do this. Hang in there," I told him.

Danquirs received more after-school help in hopes of solidifying his skills in time for the SAT. His teachers crammed in as many preparation classes as they could. Their hard work eventually paid off. He received his diploma from Phillip O. Berry Academy in 2011.

That same year Danquirs enrolled at the Art Institute of Charlotte, where he could study media arts and interactive media. He longed to work in films, and write and produce music.

Shortly afterwards, I was transferred to the Federal Correctional Institution in Jesup, Georgia. My life had changed for the better. I felt restored spiritually, and I'd turned into a man who thought he knew something about black boys. Then I reunited with someone from my past. A good friend of mine, Dr. Bruce Cox, Jr., was the head chaplain there. I shared my encounter with Danquirs. "That's your calling, Belay. You're doing something you enjoy. And besides, you are good at it," he said. That was all I needed to hear.

While in Jesup, I discovered there was no African-American man on gospel radio who was trying to build character into the lives of black boys and leave a legacy.

There was not one soul on the scene. And I realized

that if I wanted to guide more black youth from prison, I needed a platform to continue to steer them in the right direction. Sometimes you have to be the first, you have to be the one to set things in motion. Sometimes you've got to use what is available.

Something I was accustom to.

I contacted WTLD 90.5 FM, a Christian radio station in Jesup, and shared my passion with the broadcast specialist, in December 2011. I indicated that I wanted her to read my letters on the air to her young listeners. She told me, "We need more black men like you. Send whatever you have directly to me, and I'll share it." I did just that. My inspirational writings were read every Thursday evening at 6:00. So there I was again, reaching out to teenagers weekly. Eventually, I got my name out there and became popular throughout Southeast Georgia. This happened because of Anna "Sister A" Davis.

Amazed by the amount of support inside and outside of prison, I realized one could possibly incite the spark in young black men to think of themselves as assets if one truly cared about their future.

If I haven't convinced you of the importance of mentorship yet, consider this: We can only better young lives if we get involved. And we've got to start today. Tomorrow is not promised. I often daydream of building a community of black male role models. We would simply walk into fatherless homes where our black boys were at risk of dropping out of school, adopt them for the sake of our community, teach them history, and take them to museums and libraries where knowledge exists. In this fantasy, we are teaching them respect of God, self and others. Our powerful presence calms anger and pent-up rage, forces them to pull up their pants, demands accountability and responsibility. We are active. We are handling our business as men.

We are not waiting to bury more black boys before their time. We are saving our black boys and protecting their futures by any means necessary, right now.

While I don't mean to sound preachy, what better example of somebody determined to help someone in need than the Good Samaritan? The Bible tells a story of a man who was going from Jerusalem to Jericho. Some robbers attacked him. They stripped him of his clothes and beat him. Then they walked away, leaving him almost dead. A priest happened to be going down that same street. When he saw the man's condition, he refused to get involved. Then a Levite also came by. When he saw the man's condition, he refused to get involved too. But a Samaritan came to the location where the man was. When he saw the man's condition, he felt sorry for him. He went to aid him, poured oil and wine on his wounds and bandaged them. Then he assisted the man in getting on his own donkey. He took him to an inn and took care of him.

One of the reasons I love this parable is that there

are any number of teaching points to be drawn from it regarding mentorship:

1. Everyone of us have a moral responsibility to help someone in need. This includes a black boy growing up without a father, mentor or positive role model. We can't separate life from responsibility because no one can live life unless we embraces responsibility.

2. If we take the position of the priest and Levite, we will lose a generation of black boys.

3. We don't have to be a family member of an at-risk kid to reach out to him. The Good Samaritan did not know the wounded man, but he attended to his needs.

4. You must care enough about the condition of our sons to step up and do your part to save them.

5. Be a leader. We need effective plans and supportive actions to stop black youth violence.

6. God gives us many opportunities to assist young people, looking beyond ourselves to make a difference through the gifts he has giving us. Mentoring takes more than our financial resources. It takes our time. It requires the sacrifice of other things we could be doing in our spare time.

7. There's no danger in creating a stable home

environment for black boys that includes contact with a good man.

8.   Don't judge our youth. We often get caught up in "He must have been doing something he had no business doing." Everybody isn't responsible for the condition they're in. Try to be more understanding; don't put them down. That is not what mentorship is about.

9.   If you show them compassion, they will have compassion for others.

10. If we refuse to become mentors, we'll never know how many young lives we could have touched. Going back to the parable, the priest and Levite could have been a strong spiritual base for the wounded man.

My ninth grade English teacher Franklin L. Smith used to say you'll never know what you can do until you try. Too many of us are not stepping forward because we feel like we can't answer President and Mrs. Obama's national call to service. Don't refuse to serve as a mentor to some young black boy who needs a responsible caring African-American man in his life.

I've learned mentoring is not just an every-now-and-then thing. You can't just mentor a child on Christmas Day. We've got to get involved in their lives on a continuing basis. We need blue-collar mentors. We need white-collar mentors. We need religious mentors. We need you.

Are you starting to feel a little psyched out? A little like there's no danger in the water? Excellent. What I want to do next is to give you some tips on how to become a great mentor.

Who Knows Better Than You?
Why Black Men Don't Mentor

O n November 15, 2011, Mike Krzyzewski was crowned the winningest coach in men's college basketball history with 903 victories, breaking the tie with Bob Knight, his former coach at Army and his mentor throughout his professional career. Krzyewski's No. 6 Duke beat Michigan State 74-69 in the State Farm Champions Classic.

The man known simply as "Coach K" went across the court to Knight when the game ended. They were cheek to cheek in a hug. Krzyzewski, tears in his eyes, broke away and Knight pulled him back, hand on his shoulders, then one final slap of the shoulder. Their long embrace was a historic moment for all of sports; Krzyzewski, hailed as one of the athletic world's greatest leaders ever, was able to thank, and be congratulated by, the legend whose record he surpassed. How often does that happen?

"I just told coach I love him," Krzyzewski said. "I wouldn't be in this position without him. It's a moment shared. I know he's very proud and I'm very proud to have been somebody who's worked under him and studied him and tried to be like him."

Together, the two have been a factory spitting out not only great players, but exceptional ones. While Knight is most famous for his temper, it's his core principles of character and values, handed down to Krzyzewski, that have led both these coaches to the summit.

I believe that our primary job as African-American men is to live exemplary lives inside and outside our homes where black boys look up to us: Men of honor, propriety, and fortitude. Men with both composure and reserve. Men who know the value of family and faith as well as education. And our message to them should be about change and growth.

When African-American men are hesitant to guide young black males it's not because they can't. It's not because they lack restraint. I think there are other factors why African-American men shy away from being mentors:

1. They have a record.

While it is increasingly popular to take on responsibility and commitment as a volunteer in such unprecedented and somewhat skeptical times, it's my opinion that most African-American men don't mentor simply because they have a record! They did time in prison. Clearly, many of us don't have a squeaky-clean past, and so we conclude that our mentorship isn't really worth the cost of being ridiculed. We know the present condition of our boys better than anyone else, but we leave the problem for the government to fix, believing that the president is better suit for the job, that we don't have the character to affect positive change.

Most mentors out there are ex-felons. Their testimonies have been shared with thousands of kids across the country. What life has taught me is this. Simply because someone has a dark past does not mean they can't have a brighter future. Anybody can change for the better.

We as African-American men cannot dispute the fact that our boys live in a country totally ruled by women. They live in homes where either their mother, grandmother or aunt calls the shots. They attend churches where female Sunday school teachers and pastors become their authority figures. Boys need quality men who can encourage them to develop their talents. Unfortunately, the most highly visible males seem to be gangster rappers and drug dealers, both having corrupted the minds of our youth.

I am of the same opinion that being a man is more than leaving our wives husbandless, our children fatherless, our employers passionless, our families hopeless. Someone has to instill in black boys that nothing can bring them peace but themselves. Nothing can bring them peace but the triumph of principles. Who can better do this than a mentor?

2. They work long hours.

We live in a twelve hour shift society where production - and more production - seems to be the order of the day. So while African-American men see black boys go astray, as a result of absent fathers, peer pressure, and lack of role models, so often they feel their hectic work schedule will keep them from getting involved. They work from 6:00 in the morning to 6:00 in the afternoon. After a long workday, they're too exhausted and just want to sleep. There's no energy left in the tank for Bible study, the lodge, gym, or friends, much less juvenile delinquents.

But the misbehavior of black boys we gripe about so vocally isn't going to correct itself automatically. The only way to affect positive change is to give sound counsel. The Bible says, "Without the guidance of good leaders a nation falls." Somehow we've got to rearrange our schedule, set aside a couple of hours a week, and put in the service equity that will allow us to empower young lives.

3. They're not hip enough.

Some African-American men want to be involved, but they don't know how to relate. They speak at youth rallies and don't know how to connect with the audience. These men are sincere about wanting to take back their neighborhoods but when addressing the crowd, they come off as being too old school. They know nothing about Lil' Boosie or Gucci Mane. Few things are more disheartening to those who are trying to empower lives than having their fervency and firepower clumped by hip hop culture.

4. They fear the possibilities of backfire.

Some African-American men don't get involved because they are afraid of disappointing themselves and others. They wonder, "What if the kid drops out of high school? What if I'm not able to keep him from going to jail? What if I see no progress in his behavior? What if his family calls to report he ran away?"

For those interested in coaching black boys, whether they are academically challenged or high achievers, there is legitimate concern over being falsely accused of child abuse that can ruin your reputation. If you're transporting kids to a game and one of them get injured, there may be fears of liabilities, or more commonly in our contentious society, a lawsuit.

5. They don't believe anything they do will change black boys exhibiting deviant behavior.

In the sixties, as black people's consciousness was pricked by Jim Crow laws, they felt compelled to organize a non-violent movement. Today pessimism stops us dead in our tracks, preventing us from mentoring. African-American men just don't feel their efforts to save a generation of lost black boys will trickle down to where they can see positive results. Nothing is more discouraging than the feeling that nothing you can do will affect positive change anyway.

But African-American men have to stand together on a common objective. You can be an effective mentor and impact your community - if you can get over your pessimism, and your fear, and your not being hip enough, and your working long hours, and your having a record. One African-American man fighting to save a generation of lost black boys can affect positive change in their lives. And one African-American man joined by another, and another, quickly forms an alliance and, eventually, a crusade. We can affect positive change. Moreover, we must.

If One Does Not Act, One Cannot Understand

My ninth grade English teacher Franklin L. Smith used to say to me that a man will never know what he can do until he tries to do it. Chaing Kai-Shek, the former commander-in-Chief of the Army of the Chinese Revolutionary National Party, put it more succinctly: "If one does not act, one cannot understand." They were both saying, be courageous. Face the uncharted territory with boldness, believing you can handle anything that comes your way.

I believe that you've got to be fully committed to the child you mentor because if not, you're going to find yourself down the road wondering, "Why did I agree to this?," desperately searching for an excuse to walk away. Before you come into a black boy's life, make sure you're willing to be there long term, no matter what. You have to be willing to put in time and effort to establish high moral standards, teach right from wrong, stand firm against drug use and premature sexual activity, and make educational achievement non-negotiable. This is far less costly than any burial plan, drug rehab, and youth detention center.

Let me use Danquirs Franklin for an example. Although he made peace with his past, I do not let days, even weeks, go by without having real conversations with him - ones that involve me truly listening, not just teaching. As his mentor, it's my responsibility to ensure Danquirs that he has my support - whenever that is in doubt or not communicated, problems are guaranteed.

At its essence, that is what mentoring is: encouraging open discussion with others who need guidance and leaving a legacy.

In committing to a young black male you want to invest your precious time and energy leading down the right path, ask yourself what is it about this kid. What makes you say, "I see potential in him." Then ask yourself, "Am I willing to let him know the importance of having options in life? How much love, attention, and guidance I'm willing to give?"

Once you've decided that, there is another thing I encourage African-American men to do. Before signing up, you must - as we say in the hood - keep it real. What good does it do to be there long term if your heart isn't in it?

Being a mentor is about having zeal. But having

zeal with the wrong attitude is not mentorship - it's destructive. Ask yourself about the depths of your zeal for troubled black boys - without being influenced by accolades. Do you truly care enough about their future to join in the fight to save them?

Let's run through that process here. What is it about troubled black boys that touches your heart? When you hear about them being raised by struggling single mothers, do you boil over on the inside? I mean, really get hot? Do you experience strong emotion - sadness, hurt, pain - when you talk about fatherless black children or hearing something about them? Do you want to see them guided by decent African-American men who have proven that their counsel can be trusted? Are you fed up with absent fathers and deadbeat dads? All of these are indicators of your zeal, which will motivate you to become a mentor.

Now take your self-assessment deeper:

• Where does mentorship fall among the things that matter to you?

Zeal is one thing, commitment is another. Think of the great mentors of our time. They don't stand out solely because they acted on their zeal. They stand out because they remained committed to the calling they answered. Derrick Brooks did not give up on the idea of broadening inner-city children horizons through educational trips, even when youth violence was at its highest. Warrick Dunn clung to the notion of helping single mothers purchase homes, through the darkest days of the Great Recession, and today he has mobilized companies and other organizations to help furnish those homes. Tony Dungy insisted that every young athlete who messed up off the field deserved a second chance, even as he realized his position would infuriate animal rights groups, and now we all see a changed person in Michael Vick because of what he believed.

• Are you willing to set and enforce rules and values for the black boy being mentored?

When I connected with Danquirs Franklin, my objective was to become a healthy, supportive, and engaged presence in his life (and, in the nature of mentorship, to make the relationship strong). I found that listening and paying attention to Danquirs had a tendency to make me seem cool and laid back. But when I wouldn't allow the use of profanity and the N-word during our conversations, how I was perceived after that by Danquirs sometimes underwent a 180-degree about-face. Along with greater appreciation came a lot of disagreement.

Danquirs would tell me I was old-fashioned and stuck in my ways. I confronted a great deal of anger and disapproval, and it slapped me to the ground. What I learned from this is that when you become a mentor, you sometimes exchange appreciation for resentment. It is zeal and commitment that hold you steady in the face of such difficulties.

• Are you willing to show genuine interest in who the black boy being mentored is and what he cares about?

You say that black boys nowadays no longer want to respect their elders. I say that many of them feel that way because their elders stopped loving and respecting them. Show me a generation of lost black boys, and I'll show you a generation of elders responsible for losing them.

And trust me: We are losing far too many of our boys. Too many African-American men, busy with business, career, social life, personal issues, and self-indulgence, have neglected their responsibility and destroyed their relationships with their sons, leaving them to their mothers to raise - often on welfare who have strangers in and out of their lives that are in no way committed to their safety and well-being. And too many who are not fathers dismiss our boys as none of their concern. But we are learning the hard way as a society that when our boys are treated as the government's problem, they too often end up on a path of failing, victimizing, and poor choices - ultimately becoming everyone's problem.

Your involvement in the life of a black boy will pay far bigger commissions than closing the additional car sale or employee of the month recognition you could have received instead of attending his football and basketball games. Let's stop depriving black boys - and ourselves - of that same prosperity. Being present and engaged in the lives of our boys is the black agenda.

Know What's Going On
Around You And Why

If you gotten this far into this book, you must be serious about wanting to affect positive change. I've found that the first lesson in mentoring is: Know what's going on around you and why.

These days, there is almost no excuse for being uninformed of problems in the black community. After all, we live in what is called the New Information Age. Twitter reports, constantly with much faster updates than any daily newspapers. Thanks to a tweet, many of us got the news that Whitney Houston was found dead in the bathtub of her Beverly Hills hotel room. Cable news has made it possible to provide information twenty-four hours a day. Cellular telephones that once featured only special ringtones today engage us with internet access. It is ridiculous to say you have no idea of what's happening in the black community and why, because technology offers tremendous ways for us to know.

A day never goes by that I don't pick up a newspaper or watch the local news. Recently, my heart was saddened to read about two young men who messed up their lives by doing something outrageously stupid. Joshua Haynes is seventeen. Anthony Werthen is sixteen.

Both boys have a lot in common. Both are black. Both are angry. Both are from inner-city neighborhoods. Both are products of absent fathers. Both Joshua and Anthony also have one more thing in common. Both will spend a number of years in prison - the result of making bad choices.

Joshua received seven years in prison for shooting at his mother and cops responding to a fight he had with her at their home. He was charged with aggravated assault, possession of a firearm during the commission of a crime, terroristic threats and interference with government property.

Anthony's story is different, yet the same. He received ten years in prison for shooting another student in the arm. He was charged with criminal attempt to commit murder.

The prosecutor told the judge Anthony had shot the other student for "talking junk about him." He further stated to the court, "The only difference between this and a murder case is that the victim lived."

What's my point? There is an antithetical relationship between black male role models in the lives of our black boys and lawlessness in the black community. Sadly, if there's a lack of black male role models, lawlessness increases. We have too many black boys with handguns, primarily because we have too few black male role models in their lives. Lawlessness will continue to increase in black communities without black male role models because black communities without mentors able and willing to challenge youth, run off emerging street gangs and reprimand neglectful fathers are at risk. The lack of black male role models robs the neighborhoods of those little defense forces that offhandedly, but skillfully, control boys on the corner.

If role models are guides, then black boys become lost without access to them. Very often black boys are abandoned by fathers who are more interested in treating them like their nemeses than their sons. In other words, the "complaint" against black fathers is that we disown our sons and disrespect our women. Victimized by past and current sexism, lacking adequate parental skills, we deny our boys affection we were denied by our fathers, underinvest ourselves physically in their lives, creating not only social, psychological, and moral problems, but also creating identity issues. So our boys struggle with rejection. Black male role models are individuals they can connect to. They feel like we're one of them. We look like a lot of them. Some of us were raised by single mothers. Some of us lost our fathers when we were young. Some of us did not come from suburbs or gated communities.

Our generation of black boys are unloved by fathers

that are not spending quality time with them; by mothers who are cursing at them, beating them before they'll encourage them, and treating them as if they're responsible for being fatherless. There is no child - male or female, white or black - who can be held responsible for fathers that have never accepted the reality of being fathers. When a child fails in school, guess what happens? We fail as a society. Black boys are searching, and our mothers are frustrated. Simply put, they do not have the ability to effectively raise our boys.

It's hard to overemphasize the importance of mentors. Many young men have thanked me for taking interest in them.

Black boys need mentors to teach them rites of passage. Forty years ago, our boys had men to take them under their wing and show them how to change a tire and replace a glass window. How many of our boys today still experience this? How many of our boys were taught how to fish or hunt? How many of our boys had a man to take them to the doctor?

We need mentors to visit black boys who are in a juvenile detention center. We need mentors to counsel black boys who disrespect their mothers. We need mentors who can help boost black boys self-esteem and help them realize there's another path.

So let's say you've decided to mentor a particular teenage black male outside your community, but all you know about him is that he comes from a broken home. Well, you could talk with his mother to figure out where his head is at. You could ask about his goals and dreams to see what he wants to become in life. You could inquire about his decision-making skills to learn how he thinks. You could ask about his favorite hobbies; this will give you some ideas to do with him. The questions are endless. This simple approach could be taken with any fatherless child. All that's required of you is a little interest, because in all cases, probing information about a troubled youth is vital for a mentor.

Black boys want the same thing that the rest of us want: They want to be comfortable. They want a good life. But when you live in a fatherless neighborhood that's wasting away around you, your lack of structure and support makes you more vulnerable to drugs, makes you more vulnerable to an environment that is rife with crime. So we've got to take steps to touch lives, to create mentor zones, to create feeding programs.

With violence and crime too common in the black community, I believe the way to change is to reach boys needing help before they grow up and react to their circumstances.

We can't stop it now, but we can prevent it from happening in the future by reaching these kids that live in poverty-filled, drug-filled, violence-filled neighborhoods. We can prevent them from being in five years or ten years what we're hearing about on the local news now. These are the same kids.

I'm sure you all remember the saying "Twenty-five pennies, keep your nose out of other folks business."

Well, that may be valuable advice in some situations, but it is utterly wrong in reaching out to save an at-risk black boy. A fatherless child is all of our business. And twenty-five pennies is not enough to see another black boy spend a number of years in prison. They are more than a Bureau of Justice Statistic.

9/16/10

Mr. Beddick,

I received your letter. Thanks for letting me
know how much you and the other inmates
enjoyed my story about the two young men
struggling to over-come their bad childhood
experiences. You are definitely to be
commended for your determination to build
a better life for yourself when you get out
of prison. Sounds like you're on the right
path. Don't let anyone knock you off of it.
I'll tell the two young men what you've
said. Better yet, I'll just pass your letter
on to them. Thanks again for writing.

Ed Frazz

Hear 2 Listen: 6 Black Teen Summit

A re you tired of seeing black boys in your community doing nothing with themselves? Does it bother you to see them loitering in front of a business, or just hanging out on the corner? Do you want to share with them the valuable resources you gained in life? If so, it's time to present a black teen summit.

A goal is said to be the end toward which an effort is directed and accomplishing a desired outcome. In a way, this chapter is about achieving a goal. It's about knowing what works and what doesn't work when you address the needs of teenage black males.

As a grant writer instructor, I teach my students that solutions must always address the causes. This may seem self-explanatory, but all too often grant seekers will diagnose a problem appropriately but then lack the will to execute strong, comprehensive, well-developed solutions.

Here is a list of ways that can help you as you address needs of young black men at a community summit.

1. Your target audience.

Create dialogue between the black boys and a local panel. The panel can consist of teachers, city officials, pastors, corporate executives, business owners, college students, or professional athletes.

2. Befriend - don't belittle or be rude.

To win black boys over, your panel must treat them and their opinions with reason and respect, and resist the urge to demean or be rude to them. Traditional rhetoric isn't going to win over many troubled youth. Even when traditional rhetoric works, it only works in certain settings. Many of us were raised in households where we could not express ourselves. If we did, it was considered disrespect or talking back. This way of thinking will alienate a good many black boys the summit is trying to win over.

3. Ask questions.

Interest and concern are always more convincing than silences and stares. Silences only lead to more disconnect.

4. Listen.

Black boys want to be heard. My son Belay II and I had been separated from one another for nearly twelve years until recently. The separation was caused by choices I made in the past. Through persistence and determination, I located an address for him and immediately started communicating by mail. Belay II was already seventeen and extremely frank. My absence affected him greatly. There were lots of missing gaps in his life that had been filled with pain, anger, and sadness. Yet he was willing to allow me to redeem my position as his father. But not without me having to listen to how he felt growing up in a fatherless home. I was open to whatever he had to say. Some people consider this ineffective parenting from a black perspective. Listening to our sons is what some of us call a new phase of parental degeneration. Some argue that we as black men are supposed to present ourselves as disciplinarians and intimidators in the home so our sons will obey us. We're supposed to do all the talking, while our sons do the listening. They say this whole listening thing with our sons allows for fundamental necessities like respect, standard, and the disinterested obeyance of rules. My response to these grumbles is simple: The more we hear what they have to say, the more they hear what we have to say. The most effective mentors are those who know how to listen as well as address needs. Think about it: What kid wants to be talked to when he's misunderstood?

5. Make it positive.

Do whatever you can do to make taking part in your summit as positive and empowering as possible. Provide smart, deliberate, and consistent strategies for improving their lives, personally and professionally. Offer counseling. You can't lose the interest of the boys you're trying to reach. It's just not a sensible strategy. The summit should provide topics to include: high school and career preparation, peer to peer development, employability skills, youth leadership and achievement, prevention of bullying, juvenile delinquency, motivational and building self-confidence.

Has America Lost a Generation of Black Boys?

Some argue there is no longer a need for dismal prediction, fear, or anxiety about losing a generation of black boys. They feel it is too late. Very little I read shocks me. However, I must admit a recent blog on the continued erosion of our values as a race gave me quite a jolt. In education, occupation, possessions, incarceration, well-being, shelter, and child raising, it would appear we have lost a generation of young black men. The obvious question that came to mind was will we lose the next two or three generations of black boys to the concrete jungle, destructive media, gangs, drugs, ineffective teaching strategies and off-the-shelf tests, unemployment, mentor nonexistence, crime, violence and death.

The blog further disclosed that most young black men in America don't graduate from high school. Only 35 percent of black male students graduated from high school in Chicago and only 26 percent in New York City, according to a 2006 report by the Schott Foundation for

Public Education. Only a few black boys who finish high school actually enroll in college, and those few black boys who get accepted in college, nationally, only 22 percent of them finish college.

The bottom line: young black male students have the poorest grades, the lowest test scores, and the highest dropout rates of all students in the country. Do you have any idea what this mean? When these young black men don't succeed in school, they are much more likely to prosper in the nation's criminal justice and prison system. And it was determined recently that even when a young black man graduates from an American college, there is a good chance that he is from another country.

It's true that black men in prison in the United States have become as American as apple pie. I'm speaking from experience, as I approach my eighth year anniversary in the Federal Bureau of Prisons at the age of 43. There are more black men in prisons and jails in the United States (1.1 million) than there are men incarcerated in the rest of the world combined. This criminalization process now starts in elementary school with black male children as young as six and seven years old being arrested in stunning numbers according to a 2005 report, Education on Lockdown by the Advancement Project.

Worst of all is the indifference, neglect and disengagement of the black community concerning the future of our black boys. We do little while the future lives of black boys are being destroyed in record numbers. The schools that black boys attend prepare them with skills that will make them obsolete before, and if, they graduate. Outdated equipment, dilapidated building, and a host of others ills have been allowed to fester so long in schools nationwide that it seems as if expectations of success no longer exist. In a strange and perverse way, the black community, itself, has started to wage a kind of war against young black men and has become part of this destructive process.

As important as it was for me to reach out to save a black boy from prison, it should be just as critical for you and others in the community to do so. The price of procrastination is too high. Who are young black women like my daughter Brianna going to marry? Who is going to build and maintain the economies of black communities? Who is going to anchor strong families in the black community? Who will young black boys emulate as they grow into men?

Being an engaged presence in the life of a black boy is not sacrifice or hardship. Rather it is an investment in the future stability and prosperity of your community - for generations to come.

Volunteering – Giving Back To The Black Community

I f you've been taking note of the points I've offered in the previous chapters, you are well on the way to becoming a more engaged, concerned member of the black community. It all begins with your readiness to save a generation of lost black boys. So how can you get underway? What is the best way you can offer yourself? Are you a motivator or an instructor? Are you someone with more life experience than college or more college than life experience? Someone with free time but no ideas, or great ideas but little money? Are you a good reader? A good supporter? Are you a better community organizer or a better program coordinator? I talk about it all the time. If we are serious about improving the black community, we have to improve the lives of black boys. A huge piece of strategy is to get more black male role models in the nation's classroom. We all know the troubles black boys face. We know that poverty, fatherlessness, and lack of competent teachers are factors that impact our children's education.

Think about the plight and predicament of our boys and how you might best offer yourself to protect their future. Turn yourself into a black community think tank of one. Decide in what ways you can best offer yourself now, and then volunteer.

Getting Fired Up

Make inquires.

If your interest is to work to create a reading program for at-risk black boys, make inquires about existing reading programs, about available grants, about local business owners, about previous efforts. You want to be fully informed of the missed opportunities that were once available to youth in your district. Find out who else might be concerned about at-risk black boys - churches, schools, legislators, citizens. Gather the facts you discover.

Finding Resources.

Make contact with others who are interested in teaming up with you, and look for whatever valuable resources they and others can bring aboard, from influence to capital to a commitment of time. Do you need to start a grassroots organization? If so, do you have the expertise to do so - or do you need the assistance of someone who does have the expertise? Begin to create goals and objectives based on the resources - manpower, time, budget - you have available. While goals pertain to addressing issues you care about, objectives must be concrete and specific, measurable, realistic, attainable, and time-bound. If you try to design a program for at-risk boys without goals and objectives guiding you... well, hang it up. It just makes no sense.

Making Connections.

Making connections is the name of the game. It's all about finding people who can help you in your cause. Not everyone you reach out to will be interested in saving a generation of lost black boys, but they can direct you to someone who is, who knows another person who is, and so forth. Don't be afraid to ask for help.

Dr. Reddick's Tips

Of course, no two people are the same. Everyone is unique in his own special way. Here are some of the topics I've employed in my mentorship work; perhaps they will work for you also.

1. Character.

When I was young, my parents were very clear about the importance of character. "Don't pick up nothing that doesn't belong to you," my mother would preach constantly. The thought that someone might think of her as a thief or kleptomaniac was the worst thing possible. That's why she taught us to pay for whatever we wanted. She believed a person who stole couldn't be trusted.

2. Integrity.

Integrity is what you do when no one is watching; it's doing the right thing all the time, even when it may not work to your advantage. Integrity is keeping your promise. Can I count on you to come through for me? Will you put me in a bind? Do I have to call someone else?

3. Humility.

Arrogance is all about me, but assurance is a realization that God has blessed me with abilities for His divine purpose. Make sure you use your gifts to help and impact others around you.

4. Courage.

One of the most valuable lessons I learned in prison is having the courage to stand by my convictions - those things I know are godly, those guiding principles I was raised to stick with. Sometimes that means saying no when the crowd says yes. It doesn't necessarily make you popular, but at least I can walk away still feeling like a man.

5. Being a gentleman.

Today's generation of black boys desperately need help in this department, because many of our fathers either didn't hang around long or somehow thought it was appropriate to physically, verbally, and emotionally abuse a woman. And music videos and urban novels usually focus on sexual attraction, not unconditional, pure love.

6. Fatherhood.

Too many children go to sleep without their father at home, or at least without one who stays the entire night. Young black males need to know the importance of being active in the lives of their children. Research have shown that the father's relationship with his daughter will be a deciding factor in the success of her relationships with men. A girl needs her father in the home to nurture her, love her, and make her feel secure. As for a boy, if there is no father to emulate proper behavior towards a woman, he will never learn what it means to be a man or a provider.

7. Respect authority.

I was not fortunate to have my father around as a child. He passed away when I was nine, leaving my mother with a dual role. Not everything that she did or said made sense to me as a youngster, but I learned at an early age that I should respect her and that I could trust her authority as my mother, whether or not I agreed with her. After she passed away, it became increasingly clear that my best interests are those of my three brothers and four sisters were paramount to my mother, and she expected us to honor her and the decisions she made for our lives.

8. Friendship.

Friendship is not a one-way street. Too often, we appraise a friendship based on the way it profits us. But undying friendships are formed when we can cause those profits to flow toward the next person other than ourselves.

9. Taking counsel.

No one person has all the answers. My years in prison have made that painfully clear to me. Today, I am secure enough to say, "I don't know what to do." In fact, I am secure enough to say, "I need for you to break that down for me."

"I don't know what to do" is always a good acknowledgment. Especially if you need help.

"I don't know what to do - got any suggestions?" is often an even better acknowledgment.

10. The power of positive influence.

Serving prison time is tough. Just as it helps me when other prisoners encourage and lift me up, I know that they need that as well.

Life experience has taught me no matter where a person is in their life's journey, they can begin today to be very deliberate about leaving a pathway of positive memories in the lives of those around them.

11. Powerful thoughts.

Our lives will be affected by how much we allow the things around us - like a setback - to affect the direction of our journey. We will never be able to do anything about removing all the perplexities we find along the way. The key is to continue to center our thoughts on where we want to be, regardless of those perplexities.

12. Education.

It all starts with a book. Harper Lee, a descendant of Robert E. Lee and author of *To Kill a Mockingbird*, once said, "Until I feared I would lose it, I never loved to read. One does not love breathing." Most of us can play sports, but do we have the reading skills necessary for competing with an ever-changing society? Make sure that you do everything in your power to give yourself that chance.

I never pretend to have all the answers for troubled black boys. However, I believe these topics will help them think about where they're headed. We have to start somewhere.

Do Your Best

Do your best. Let me repeat that. Do your best. This is never asking too much. Besides isn't that what life is all about anyway? Doing your best means you are determined to inspire a black boy and affect positive change in his life. The one way you can guarantee success is if you keep trying. You've got to believe in yourself, and the black boy you're helping, and lead.

In your eagerness to get going, there are bound to be some hard-core doubters ready to discourage you. The first thing they'll try to do is tell you what can't be "done." You don't know how rambunctious at-risk boys can be, they'll say. You're out of your league.

You have to learn to brush aside your doubters. You have to block out their negative comments with your own positive affirmation of working with a black boy. Anyone mentoring a young black male in America generally has to answer one basic question: why.

Why?

Why are you passionate about black boys? That late afternoon, as I read the story about Danquirs Franklin and Juwon Lewis, young black males had the highest dropout rates of all students in the country. That reality sat, a discernible, vexing demon, in the cell with me, strode along the asphalt track on the recreation yard, lay in wait for me in the food line. That statistic, like so much else in black America, is implausible, disturbing, and ridiculous. Somewhere between the fact that black boys are the prime victims of adult male neglect and abandonment, and the myth that they are broken or that they have a genetic flaw, lies the truth. But why should you find it?

Having two black sons of my own, I am obligated to groom my children into becoming future role models to a community of boys who will look up to them. I am no expert on fatherhood, my home cluttered with portraits of the perfect family. I can honestly say my sons, De'Andre and Belay II, are getting the right message about what it means to be a man in this world, about how they should live and pray and talk and respect others. A lot of our boys are getting the wrong message, and we as mentors need to put an end to that.

I often think about my legacy. Yes, you read it right. In one of his sermons, Martin Luther King preached about wanting to be remembered for trying to help somebody. Ultimately, he left us a legacy of civil rights.

So when you hear doubters say, "Them kids ain't

going to listen to nobody; They're too far gone," tell them - and most important, tell yourself - "They never met anyone like me."

I'd like to leave you with a verse from one of my favorite hymns of the church, "*A Charge to Keep I Have*":

> To serve this present age, my calling to fulfill
> May it all my powers engage to do my
> Master's Will.

It is the will of God that we inspire black boys and affect positive change in their lives.

Letters From Danquirs Franklin

October 18, 2010

Dear Belay,

    First and foremost, I want to thank you for your support. Please forgive me for the late response. Eric kept forgetting to give me the letter you wrote him. I didn't get it until two weeks ago. When I read it, I was touched and speechless by the things you wrote. I had no idea that me and Juwon's story affected so many lives.

The other day, I remember telling my family and friends how I was giving people something to live for. We all need encouragement.

I want to recommend a book for you to read. It's called The Color of Water: A Black Man's Tribute to His White Mother by James McBride. Until next time, keep your head up.

Sincerely,

Danquirs

December 19, 2010

Dear Belay,

   I am glad to know that you received your Christmas card and letter. Like I expressed in my last letter, I'm trying to keep hope alive. Some of our people have giving up on life. I refuse to do so. My future is bright.

   Things are great here in Charlotte. And the family is doing well, also. I have some good news to tell you. I found out that Juwon lives not too far from me. We ran into each other on Friday at the store. Our conversation was brief because he was on the move. I can say this much about him. He appears to be doing well.

   I want you to know that my grandmother and mother love the

letters you wrote them. We all consider you to be part of the family, especially me.

So your son De'Andre will be graduating this school year? That's great! We need more black males to graduate and make something of themselves.

Now to answer your question. No, I have never been to Tampa. However, I plan to visit there one day. A friend of mine lives down there. He's a schoolteacher.

Let me say this before I end this letter. I want to thank you because it's not often I get a wonderful person from prison to write me. I really appreciate everything you are doing. Until next time, may God be with you.

Sincerely,

Danquirs

P.S. In your next letter tell me
everything about you.

January 13, 2011

Dear Belay,

　Your letter was very touching. I really enjoyed learning about you and your life. You are family to us, and we love having you. I just want to say Happy Birthday. Keep your head up.

Love,

Danquirs

P.S. My birthday is February 19.

February 25, 2011

Dear Belay,

How are you doing? I am doing okay in school. God blessed me to pass all my class exams this first semester. The second semester isn't going to be hard either.

I am glad you liked your birthday card. My birthday is on Saturday. I'll be 19-years-old, on my way becoming a man.

Did you go for Green Bay in the Super Bowl? I love the Packers. It's green and yellow in this household.

I'm curious. If you could be a super hero, who would it be and why? I like the Wolverine. Until next time, keep you head up.

Much Love,

Danquirs

March 10, 2011

Dear Belay,

How is life treating you? Me, I am okay. Occasionally, I have my ups and downs like everyone else my age. Other than that, I am still living.

Thanks for the birthday card. I can't believe I'm 19. My mother says that I am before my time, which is true, but that's a conversation for another day.

I didn't do much on my birthday. I received $60.00 and had three different cakes. A Chocolate Cake. A Cheese Cake. A Carrot Cake. I'm supposed to get a tattoo. We'll see. Until next time, keep your head up.

Love,

Danquirs

April 25, 2011

Dear Belay,

How was your Easter? I had a good one. My mother and grandmother prepared fried chicken, baked chicken, greens, lima beans and rice. I also spent the day with my homeboy Jason, cousins and baby mama.

Did I tell you that we have a baby on the way? My girl is three months pregnant, but that's a story for another time.

The folks are doing fine. And no, I didn't take any pictures on my birthday. It was a good one, although I never got that tattoo. I might get it later.

If you're wondering, yes, I have started backing playing basketball. So that's a plus, right? And you're

absolutely correct by saying I am
my own hero. Until next time, Keep
your head up.

Much love,

Danquirs

February 1, 2012

Dear Belay,

I am still in school and working at the comedy club. To be honest, I feel like crap right now. I just lost two beautiful young women that I was in love with. I hurt both of them bad, especially my baby mama. It's all good.

So everybody knows about me down in Jesup, Georgia? WOW! I had no idea that my story was still out there for conversation. After all, it has been nearly two years since The Charlotte Observer did the story on me and Juwon.

Keep doing the work of the Lord. Obviously, He is on your side because the young people are listening to you. Until next time, keep your head up.

Much Love,

Danquirs

P.S. Happy Belated Birthday!

February 25, 2012

Dear Belay,

It seems like our dreams are coming true. My mother and I gave the world a story like no other. And now you're trying to share yours, too. I knew God allowed us to connect for a reason. It was obvious. Think about it. I was in Charlotte, North Carolina and you were in Edgefield, South Carolina when The Charlotte Observer ran my story. God knew you had a passion for young black men struggling to learn about manhood. He also knew I was one of them. So He allowed our paths to cross at a pivotal point in our lives.

Because of you, I can see that sky box much clearer now. I had a dream you helped me to become a millionaire before I reached the age of 30. Funny, huh?

I believe in you just like you believe in me. It's all about making a difference. This is just the beginning. Until next time, Keep your head up.

Much Respect,

Danquirs

P.S. I feel old being 20 (Smile)

Epilogue

Every sentence is a sense of urgency. Each paragraph is a strategy; each page, an outline plan. I wrote about mentorship because at this moment there is no topic more essential to address, more important to advocate. Until I wrote about black men becoming mentors, I could not preach or think or dream of anything else behind this razor wire fence.

The possibility of hope had guided my pen in writing this book. Hope, like some new medical breakthrough is now available to us. And if we love black boys and ourselves, we must be willing to share this message of hope with them collectively and individually.

But an unquenchable thirst for, and lifetime commitment to mentorship has fueled these words. We criticize and knock the black men who are not stepping into their leadership and vainly waiting for someone else to reach our boys. What will we do to honor and help the ones who are?

If the daily indifferences toward responsibility, mature masculinity, and well-being that predominate pockets of the black community were attitudes directed at our boys by men of any other race, these feelings would be considered hatred. How else to view it when African-American men who leave their sons trying to figure out manhood alone. Reading Danquirs and Juwon's story that afternoon with watery eyes, perhaps saddened by the fact that no adult black male was there for them, I sincerely prayed for God to revamp areas of my life that were not me. For I, too, had failed both boys, was in the first year of my sentence. I knew that the sentiments of contempt, hostility, and bitterness brewed in my heart would inspire me to become an advocate.

Experience has thought me silence is not going to encourage young men at-risk and affect positive change in their lives. Men willing to let them know the importance of having options in life will. At the end of the day, we have an obligation, we are responsible for what we do, and our communities will judge us, accordingly.

Of course, in the most ultimate, far-reaching sense, it is only recruiting of black male role models that will guarantee the success of our boys. All the most objective and uniformly respected studies have found, year after year, that black boys, raised by single mothers, poorly educated, not exposed to mentors, will not succeed at the highest levels. Danquirs and Juwon, like all of America's fatherless black boys, pays a "default tax" for the no-shows of their dads at the altar. I am agonized and annoyed confronting that reality. Fatherless black boys are too.

The influence and power of black male role models have been essential and valuable beyond measure simply because they have chosen to give up certain things in order to build into the lives of young black men. They are able to look beyond themselves to affect positive change.

It's possible for you, too. Black boys need guidance, and you can offer that, from your past mistakes and experiences in life. Trust me; there is a black boy out there who needs to know that you love him enough to insist, to demand, to require, that he succeed.

Q & A With Dr. Reddick

Q: Is there a way to remedy the shortage of black men and increase the number of good ones?

A: Research has shown 3 percent more black boys are born at birth than black girls. Eighteen years later there are 80 percent more available black women than men. If a single black female wants a black male who is honest, spiritual, loving, and faithful the proportion is more like 5 to 1. Black men are found in much greater numbers in graveyards, penitentiaries, court ordered drug outpatient treatment and anger management programs, unemployed or unemployable, interested in non-black women, and on the down low. It is estimated that in another eight years, 70 percent of all black males will be unavailable.

I do not believe the reason this problem exists is complex and interwoven between white male superiority, overt prejudice, and institutional racism substantiated by black apathy and ignorance. Our boys live in households totally ruled by women, and they're not around quality men who can encourage them to develop their talents.

The lack of good men will continue to hurt generations and generations of black boys. A way to correct the shortage of adult black males and increase the number of good ones is by mentoring young black men. A black boy without a positive role model in his life only cripples the African-American community.

Q: Is it true that incarcerating black males cost more than sending them to college?

A: Yes. Many people are unaware that it costs $10,000 for a four year degree, and $24,000 annually for a prison bed. Yet Republicans want to cut Pell grants for college, and allocate more federal funds to build more prisons. America seems to value incarceration more than education.

Q: How can we reduce the number of black males dropping out of high school?

A: I favor community education zones where single black mothers and their sons receive support services that boost a fatherless student's chance of being successful in school. Many inner-city neighborhoods with education zones have attained strong results, including a graduation rate of more than 90 percent for black males.

Q: You want to develop a black male youth clinic in

several cities nationwide. Can you describe the proposed services of that clinic?

A: I'm envisioning a clinic that works with black boys ages 9-17. Progressive black men would be staffed to teach them what a man's responsibilities are. Many teenage black males do not appreciate the value of husbandhood and fatherhood, which is the true essence of manhood.

Q: How can we encourage black men to become more involved in the lives of black boys?

A: More and more cities are seeing an increase in black-on-black crimes. When you ask the perpetrators to explain their actions they blame it on being disrespected.

In my monthly newsletter, *All Pastors Bulletin*, I offer African-American pastors all across the nation various strategies for stopping the vicious cycle of violence and murders that is crippling the black community. Not many people are aware of the mentality that gives rise to destructive behavior among young black men. With many years of experience in research, program planning and evaluation, operating a nonprofit organization, and conducting free professional grant writing classes in basic proposal writing, it is my conclusion that the black church is central to the black community, and the best institution to help those young males find their place in the world.

In an attempt to encourage black men to become mentors, we need to do awareness campaigns. It should include an aggressive marketing drive across television, radio, print publications and the Web. Churches could work with Nike or Reebox marketing execs, who can volunteer their services, as well as with professional athletes, who can appear in public service announcements.

The primary goal should be to highlight the great sense of purpose and fulfillment that comes from being a positive role model.

Q: What are the rites of passage programs about?

A: There are approximately 50 rites of passage programs being ran across America. These programs work with black boys on a continuing, steady basis and teach them the benchmarks for manhood. Upon successful completion of a program, the boys participate in an emotional ceremony in front of their peers, family, and the larger community. The rites of passage program established minimal standards of what the program coordinators felt boys needed for manhood in order to receive this honor. These benchmarks include: understanding of African cultural, spirituality, economics, politics, community involvement, charity, physical development, and belief in the Nquzo Saba, a black value system.

Q: How can we do a better job teaching black boys to be responsible?

A: First and foremost, single black mothers have to stop telling their eleven-year-old sons, "You're the man of the house." I believe manhood is earned and not given.

We should start very early and encourage the development of responsibility about being on time, personal hygiene, clothes, room upkeep, chores, games and equipment, earning an allowance, studying, and of course, sexuality. It's useless to start at fifteen when black boys have already made babies.

Q: How do you motivate black boys?

A: All black boys are motivated by something. They may not be motivated in academics, but many are extremely motivated to wear Ture Religion Jeans, drive Cadillac Escalades with 30 inch rims, play in the NFL, and become the latest Drake.

It's very difficult to be a lawyer if you have never been around one. When I was in high school, I had a summer job working for a great attorney in Jacksonville, Florida named Earl M. Johnson. This job was offered to me through a program known as Career Beginnings. Our boys need positive black male role models to interest them in achieving academically. They get more opportunities to meet role models in sports and entertainment than they do English and history. Interestingly, I used to be a GED tutor and the younger federal prisoners in my class were not motivated in writing essays; however, they did extremely well in participating in open class discussions. I understood that they did so well in debates because they were motivated - they were good at expressing themselves, and felt more comfortable doing so verbally than on paper. Schools need to promote academic achievement the way they do with athletic achievement. We must also help black boys find their God-given talents so they can increase their self-esteem.

Q: How do you get black boys to appreciate long-term gratification over short-term gratification?

A: Everyday I meet young black men in the system that rather take their chance again to sell crack cocaine when they get out and face another ten years than work a 9 to 5 job making minimum wages, and remain free.

Young black men feel they can make a million dollars faster in selling drugs, committing bank fraud, sports, music industry, and the lottery; those five areas have become our competition.

We have to show black boys there are better odds in the academic arena than there are in drugs, sports, theft, music, and the lottery. For example, black boys hear drug dealers get plenty of money but rarely do they hear drug dealers get plenty of time. We need to take them to United States Penitentiaries, drug rehabs, intensive care units, and morgues. We must have them name all the people they know who have been selling drugs and went to prison then add their time up together.

Long-term gratification does not mean you suffer for years before you begin to see the fruit of your labor. There can be short-term triumphs. I think we as black men need to provide them to our boys at regular interims, to encourage them to resist the onslaught of materialism currently being experienced by their drug dealing peers.

Q: What are your feelings about an evening cultural school?

A: I wish my community had one when I was growing up. The African-American community is too dependent on public schools to do so much for black boys: feed them breakfast and lunch, teach them during the school day, make sure they act right, and provide counseling and after school programs. I would like to see schools teach culture and history to our boys from an African frame of reference, but we need to do this ourselves. I repeat, I wish my community had one when I was growing up.

Q: Can you describe Partnership for Prevention and Guidance?

A: Partnership for Prevention and Guidance is compromised of advocates for social reform and African-American male professionals who are concerned about youth violence and the high school dropout rate. Our mission is to help train youths on issues of conflict to avoid, and let them know about the value of education in their lives.

I formed this national movement after the Trayvon Martin and George Zimmerman incident. The group's current priority is to stop kids from being recruited into gangs by offering them training, education, and an opportunity to build a legitimate life. Like us at PartnershipForPreventionAndGuidance on Facebook.

About the Authors

Belay D. Reddick, Sr., D.D., former pastor of First Baptist Church in Immokalee, Florida, is a mentor coach and urban community strategist. In addition, Dr. Reddick's inspirational and motivational open letter to young black men has been heard weekly on Augusta's 103.7, the former home of The Helen Blocker-Adams Show, and Jesup's 90.5, home of The Anna Davis Hour, local Christian radio stations with a combined listenership of three hundred fifty thousand. Partnership for Prevention and Guidance, his national grassroots initiative, connects fatherless African-American boys with adult black male mentors. The father of three children, Dr. Reddick is one of the most noted youth advocates in the Federal Bureau of Prisons. He serves time at the Federal Correctional Institution in Miami, Florida.

Danquirs Franklin is a student at the Art Institute of Charlotte, where he studies media arts and interactive media. He plans to work in films and write and produce music. Danquirs lives with his mother and grandmother in North Carolina.

www.ingramcontent.com/pod-product-compliance
Lightning Source LLC
Chambersburg PA
CBHW050416290526
45786CB00003B/1293